Praise for *Red Thread Thr*

I love these poems. Love is the v

much too pallid to convey the luminous quality of the
imagery, the straight-at-you honesty and candor of the
subjects, the precise, often rapier-sharp quality of the
language. These are not poems for the timid, capturing
as they do the paradoxical intertwining of domestic and
mythic, intimate and philosophical, keenly observant
and musingly imaginative. These are poems for the
times-in-between, when the way home winds a bit too
crookedly, or when the fog rolls in too thick and fast.
Gay's poems are gifts for all of us in need of a phrase
like "Don't you see the whole world shining?" Exactly
that.

—Ronne Hartfield,
poet and author of *Another Way Home*

"I've got a poem stuck in my shoe," writes Gay Guard-
Chamberlin in her poem "Hitchhiker." Thankfully for
us, the poet shares her pearls. In this collection Guard-
Chamberlin witnesses climate change and migraines,
laments aging body parts, grimaces over politics, and
finds joy in ordinary things like coffee and paper clips.
She pays tribute to all the important people in her life,
including "the kitchen witch"—her mother—by
questioning their authority while paying homage to it.
Her words are as lucid as "incandescent rain." Reading
them is like eating up the stars.

—Caroline Johnson,
poet and author of *The Caregiver*

Guard-Chamberlin's poems are witty and contemporary comments on modern life modulated by heart-felt homages to others. The poems about her mother are full of love, anger, and forgiveness. I enjoyed the political poems in a different way. Truly, there is something for every reader here.

—Elizabeth Kerlikowske,
poet and author of *Art Speaks*

Red Thread Through a Rusty Needle

Poetry

by

Gay Guard-Chamberlin

NEW WIND
PUBLISHING

New Wind Publishing | Sacramento

Guard-Chamberlin, Gay
Red Thread Through a Rusty Needle: poems / by Gay Guard-Chamberlin
p. cm.
1st ed.
ISBN 978-1-929777-12-9
LCCN 2019913619
        I.   Title.
811'.54—dc22

Published in the United States by
New Wind Publishing
5315 Spilman Avenue
Sacramento, California 95819
www.newwindpublishing.com

Printed in the United States of America

Cover design by Karen Phillips/PhillipsCovers.com
Author photo by Lucia Lombardi
Logo design by Jim Hunt

Dedicated to my father Sam Guard
with much appreciation for his engineer's mind
and his poet's heart.

RED

giddy up girl

remember back when you were a
giddy gritty city girl
your head packed full of books
full of horse love
not much horse sense
                    giddy up and yippee ki yay

tamed and gentled
well-trained well-bred
stuck in the car carsick
nothing to do
nowhere to be
nothing to see

but a herd of relatives
in the front seat recounting the dead
remember how you pressed
your hot face
to cool green grass
counting off tree grass rock cloud
                    whoa nelly slow down

something moved up a hill
whirling swirling red dust
danced in the air
fast as a shot
wild horses running
running for their lives
galloping a mantra you memorized
                    they are real they are real they are real

the chant ran on and on
like horses no one else saw
you quick-folded the moment
                    equus caballus abracadabra

hid it in your secret pocket
waited for your own untamed life
to begin

THE REGULARS

As usual, Regret arrives
hand in hand with Dread —
what a well-dressed pair
argyled in grey and red.

Chronic complainers, they demand
attention even before sitting down:
frou-frou drinks, the appetizer plate,
an urgent second round.

Other patrons beckon with a wave,
the lofted empty coffee cup,
but how can I escape when
they're just warming up:

The meal? Tasteless. Portions?
Meager. And from where
is that awful draft coming?
Surely a better table's over there,

and how can anyone even think
with all this lunch crowd racket?
The list goes on and on,
they threaten to pack it,

take their business elsewhere,
but since this little drama is repeated
every time they dine,
I know they'll be back again, undefeated,

my regulars, Dread and Regret,
making a beeline for my station,
armed with their pretense of a good tip:
last week's *Your Daily Inspiration.*

STELLA MARIS

High above the North Pole is the Stella Maris, Star of the Sea. High above the North Pole is an eye that looks down the spine of the world. Without this light from the Stella Maris we would be flung into a corner of the universe, shattered and forgotten.

Stella was my grandmother's name and her undying shame. Tennessee Williams ruined it for her, she said, and she never forgave him, or Marlon Brando either. Stella wore muumuus from Hawaii and Evening in Paris perfume. She had feather shoes and seashell purses.

Nobody was allowed into my grandmother's room before noon. She looked like an alien queen sleeping in her enormous bed, surrounded by her five dogs and four cats. Stella didn't wear nightgowns or pajamas; she wore negligees and little ruffled black negligees over her eyes to keep out all the light. Her fuzzy slippers purred by the side of the bed where her blind feet could find them.

My grandmother had hundreds of eyes on the ends of her fingers. If she got woken up too soon, her arms would break into ten thousand pieces and fall to the floor, an incandescent rain.

My grandmother dated Johnny Weissmuller before he went to Hollywood and became Tarzan. Dating Johnny meant going to the 92nd Street YMCA and watching Johnny swim. Stella sat with her arms folded in her lap, watching Johnny's strong arms slice the turquoise water. He smelled of chlorine. He swam back and forth, forth and back. Her eyes were blinded by the turquoise light. The motion of his crescent arms lulled her to sleep.

The sound of the television woke her up. She saw her four grandchildren bathed in turquoise light, watching Johnny Weissmuller swimming across the screen in black and white, back and forth, forth and back.

So little is known anymore of the divine Sea Mothers who lived deep in the ocean, in the *bit muumu*, the womb-chamber. The divine Sea Mothers made statues out of mud, breathed into their mouths, and brought them to life.

My grandmother took baths so hot she was hidden inside thick white clouds. She had powders and potions, lotions and oils in different colored bottles. She could change water into silk, into blood, into milk.

"Grandma, are you in there?" "Yes my darling, here I am. Come in here so I can kiss you. You look good enough to eat! I'm going to eat you all up. Come here so I can pinch you and poke you. I will stroke you and strike you and give you some little sweet thing to eat."

Stella loved to read and she read everything — cookbooks, dictionaries, cans of dog food — but her most favorite things were detective novels, mysteries, spy thrillers. She always knew how it would come out before she started because she always read the ending first. She read from back to front like every book was a Torah. Stella lay inside the milky clouds she made reading her books backwards while the pages curled and the covers rippled and the words dripped down through the water.

My grandmother, the Star of the Sea, had four strawberry plants growing on the windowsill above the bathtub. The strawberries grew fat and juicy in the hot steamy room. The vines wrapped down the cool tiled walls. The vines curled up to her mouth and fed her their sweet red fruit. She swallowed the berries and the little black seeds sprouted inside her. When she opened her mouth, strawberries tumbled out. My grandmother fed me strawberries that she grew inside her.

Stella had a sweet tooth that made her get up in the middle of the night searching for some little sweet thing to eat or drink. One night, reaching to pluck the ripest berry that hung high in the sky, she fell and she laid on the bathroom floor for three days and nights, floating on the cold tiles. Her strawberry plants grew down and covered her with their leaves.

Her father, who died when she was a baby, came by in a small boat. His boat was a cradle that rocked her to shore. He smoothed back her hair and kissed her forehead and gave her a book. It was a book she had lost long, long ago. It was a book she had forgotten she had ever owned, a beautiful book, an exquisitely beautiful book. It fit just right into her hands and the cover sparkled like a jewel. It was written in the ancient language of her forgotten Gypsy ancestors and it told her all the stories of all the people who came before. She read it from back to front and front to back.

Stella picked the strawberries and spread them on the pages and licked up all the sweet words. She swallowed the book and the little black seeds of letters sprouted inside her. When she opened her mouth, invisible words tumbled out. My grandmother fed me the sweet invisible words she grew inside her.

When she was taken to the hospital, the doctors emptied all the blood from her body and put her in a large fish tank so she could breathe through her gills. As to the cause of her continuing phosphorescence, little is understood. It has been speculated that the curiously erratic light phenomena are subject to the will of the creature and determined by the shapes of the constellations. A constellation is any pattern of stars that have fallen from the ceiling and grown on the floor of the ocean.

Stella Maris is another name for Isis... Stella Maris is another name for Ishtar... is another name for Venus... another name for Mother Mary... another name for Aphrodite... another name for the Grand Mother... for grandmother... another name... another... an Other... Stella is... Stella.

IN MEMORIAM

Stovetop meal refrigerator art
woozy wheels on the rolling cart
woman in the oven liar liar
biting stench of hair on fire
splatter pattern on the floor
overdone roast guests at the door
skewer them with curse and quip
a pound of Dorothy Parker's wit
the gist of the matter is the marrow
the house thin cold and narrow
truth be told in gristle and bone —

she threw in her towel too soon.

CORPORAL

Home the hero
goes down the dark
stairs to his cellar
tears old shirts into useful rags
lays his tools along the spine
of his trusted sawhorse.

Hammer axe
wrench pliers
drill nailgun awl
screwdriver jack
he buffs them sonsabitches
to a high-gloss shine.

Home the hero
climbs the dark
stairs out to the backyard
crumpling the day's
already rotten news
with his fists.

Home the hero
tosses the papers
into a rusty tin tub
splashes in a dash
of high-flash kerosene
and a goddamned handy

strike-anywhere match.

POST-ELECTION MANIFESTO

Distraught depressed yes
but do not fret
dear friends.

We will not be dissuaded
disenfranchised dissed
demeaned dispossessed
or denied.

Dispel fear.
Disseminate hope.
Dare to dispense truth
instead.

Stay disgusted with injustice
keep sharp your healthy
distrust of deceit.

Remember your roots
remember that everything
has roots.

Even the word *courage*
is from the heart
and has *rage* as its taproot.

Do not let go
of your fine strong outrage.
Keep it close and well-fed
from your own red raw
electric pulsing
beautifully full
ever-overflowing

Bleeding Heart.

FORECAST, A TO Z

Are we anti-anteater? Do we abhor the aardvark?
   Are we that
Bored with bees and buffalo?
Catastrophic climate change is un-
Deniable and yet doesn't officially
Exist. Must we extinguish every ecosystem on
Earth?
Forever is how long they're
Gone, it's the unimaginable
Hell no one wants to
Imagine, but let's do it, let's envision this world
   without
Jaguars or jellyfish, without jackrabbits and jays.
Keep picturing your own
Life without the delight of knowing there are
Marvelous monkeys playing in trees.
No more trees. No more
Otters, no octopus, no orangutan — the Orange
People, the natives call them, reminding us to
Question all authority except that of Nature.
Radically-rooted
Sustainability is what's needed now.
There's no time to
Undo, no time before we reach the Uncanny
Valley.
We are the condition that must change or it will be:
X marks the spot where the last one died, and
Your name on the bottom line as the countdown
   goes to
Zed. Zilch. Zip. Zero.

THE INNER LIFE OF WORDS

Take *heart,*
for instance,

how *h* and *t*
bookend either side

of the middle
where *ear* resides,

a clue hidden
in plain sight to

remind us
Something is

always there,
listening,

from the heart
of the heart.

THREAD

HITCHHIKER

I've got a poem
stuck in my shoe.
Pesky pebble of a notion
it nips at heel, then toe,
dogs my every step, insists
I slow, then stop, take stock
of what it is — and what it's not.

Hobbled, I kneel,
bend head and knee,
unlace humbled tongue,
pull foot from shoe,
send in hand instead.
My five-fingered search team
spelunking the dark will ferret out
the bit that bites, hold it up to light.

Is this one to keep, a nugget
I might polish to a shine
in the busy rock-tumbler
of my mind, or only a crumble of earth,
some detritus to discard?

No matter. Even cast aside,
stone-poems never die.
Patient as moss,
persistent as thistle,
they lie in wait,
ready to hitch a ride
with the next fool-poet
hoofing it down the street.

AFTER HEARING OF YOUR SUICIDE

I thought the afternoon quite pleasant
the day we stopped for a bite to eat,
a chance to chat about this and that,
but now I spend my time searching for clues
in how you looked and what you said.

Did I notice? Did I listen?
Or did I lean my head
at the right angle to convey attention,
then place a bookmark between your words
so my mind could wander off in the woods instead?

Maybe I missed a cue, or my version
was a poor translation, or a page fell out
of that edition, or the stars were not aligned.
Perhaps I was distracted by the articulation
of the hooks upon which you hung
your advanced education,

or I was wondering if the exact color
of your hair and mood matched
or clashed with your decor,
or where we could have coffee next time,
or if tea would be the better solution,

but most likely I was searching
through my tattered box of memories
for a few reliable recipes to share —
herbal tinctures used to sew
up sleep's torn pockets,
or that other one I used to know by heart —

how to bake good intentions into bread.

20

SHIFT CHANGE

Even in this city, and not so long ago,
one could still hear the shift change
as dusk began to seep into daylight.

Bands of swallows and twilight bats
swooped and flickered, their susurrations
lending shadow and murmur to the coming night.

Street lamps would flit on and off, fitful,
forgetful, an erratic glimmer along darkened
streets neon-lit by a few small shops.

Traffic was a far-away background sound,
no louder than the lake throwing itself
endlessly against its well-worn rocks.

And from my bedroom window
I could hear Old Owl lament
her fast-approaching final flight,

and I felt I knew what she meant.

EAT UP THE STARS

— for Doug

When my dog takes me dancing
showing off his finest hair suit
his David Bowie eyes
his best bespoke manners
with matching bowtie
everyone watches us

Ginger & Fred
our way across the ballroom floor
the high curve of his tail
pointing up to the moon
but when his ears fold back like fans
I know he's distracted

by a secret faraway music
from distant burrow & den
let's go he whistles let's run
past houses & fields
through woods like wind
until we can't run anymore

fall down on deer grass
eat up the stars.

THE PARK CLOSES AT NIGHT

The Park, always polite but punctual,
sweeps its last human visitors onto the sidewalk.
A bit bewildered, we head home, unaware
of the trees singing soft green lullabies
as they brush out each other's branches
with their tender twig-fingers.

The busy clans of tree-dwellers
stop their bird-bickering and squirrel-squabbling,
get about the business of closing up shop.
How industrious they all are working together,
beak and paw, wing and jaw,
rolling back the grass like a big tarp,
tucking in every little violet
and toadstool for the night.

Thistleheads and sturdy Prairie grasses
reach up, catch the hem of dark,
pull it down like an old blanket,
tattered and torn,
for the spiders to mend.

Soon, all is hushed,
nimble muskrats and resident raccoons
the only ones left with a job to do:
embossing the first-to-be-seen
evening stars with new silver threads.

THE CAUSE OF CROWS

Hey!
    Hey.
        Hey you
        down there.
                I'm talking to you.

Listen now. I can tell you about finding things.

    I'm a certified expert.

My kind are jack-of-all-trades
collectors & cataloguers
clever curators of clutter.

Who did you *think* invented the knickknack shelf?

Here's what I have so far:

1 brass hinge
plastic soldier, missing head
8 acorns
4 really good twigs
3 earrings (1 red, 1 turquoise, 1 clear as water)
1 crab claw
1 dime
2 nails plus rust
1 mouse skull
green button with black thread, dangling
2 more good twigs

So how about you?

What have you found today?

Hey
hey HEY!

Stupid wingless two-legs

don't you see

this whole world

shining?

REFORMATION

When my recently divorced neighbor announced
she was a virgin — again — I thought, *What an ass,*
but, in fact, she was not the only Mary-wannabe
in her mega-church women's bible study class.
A pastor-doctor with some doctored-up doctrines
had convinced them he could change the past.

Hymnal in hand, he rendered them whole,
with an option for an operation to rebind
the long-gone hymen, to seal the cave door.
Over the threshold of space and time
he shepherded his bleating flock,
ferrying old skins, new wine.

Please understand my scorn, these folks
were quite extreme. And did I mention
they banned books, deemed art obscene?
On their fast track to redemption,
their plans for tree-worshippers (like me)
were filled with malignant intentions.

But now, with so many friends and family
gone, so many of my days already spent,
I actually kind of get what it was
those foolish born-again maidens meant,
for who among us doesn't wish for a do-over,
the George Bailey fix, a heaven-sent

friendly angel to come down and say, *Yes, yes.*
Until now it's only been a test, a dress
rehearsal. If only I could spool everything back
like a Nautilus shell, mending every past mess
(my first kiss, the relations I pissed, opportunities
    missed)
and return renewed, reformed, refreshed,

remade, ready for my encore life —
seams straightened, broken zippers replaced,
holes darned with heavy-duty thread,
shoes reheeled and shining, aglets laced,
carrying, over the threshold of time and space,
a wiser me with a younger face.

TIE A HANGMAN'S ROPE AROUND YOUR HEAD

— old remedy for migraine

From a rope across my forehead
I pull an extra-wide moving van
hauling

cast-iron pots
dirty dishes
clocks that stopped long ago
laundry to be folded
overdue library books
leaky garden hoses
unfinished paintings
muddy hiking boots
half a manuscript
dead relatives stuffed into pillows
faded silk flowers
old news
an entire Mariachi band

my favorite grove of willow
burned down to ash.

BOOK CLUB

My mother & I have a book club.
It meets on one side of death,

then the other.
When we meet at my place,

I give her bagels & lox,
peppery iced black coffee.

She says, Not like New York,
but it'll do.

When I go to her house, she serves me
from the big white cracked family platter.

Nothing on it but raw onion, cut so fiercely
my tears cry themselves.

MY MOTHER'S KEEPSAKES

I have kept my mother's shadow
On a hook behind the door
It whispers quiet like a cape
Draped around my shoulders

On a hook behind the door
A necklace my father made her
Draped around my shoulders
Blue stones made of evening rain

A necklace my father made her
Scent of marigold still lingers
Blue stones made of evening rain
Her lullabies they remember

Scent of marigold still lingers
Four dried-out brushes in a jar
Her lullabies they remember
Driftwood and a yellowed candle

Four dried-out brushes in a jar
Red thread through a rusty needle
Driftwood and a yellowed candle
Her empty canvas on an easel

Red thread through a rusty needle
It whispers quiet like a cape
Her empty canvas on an easel
I have kept my mother's shadow.

RUST

EASTER EGGS FOR LUNCH

— for my brother & sisters

I remember how we four
liked to crack each hunt's

hard-won hoard against
our hard-boiled heads, and

the year the yolk was on us —
like a magician's trick

the sleight of hand was
seen at last while we stared

at one another paired
across the dining table,

gooey raw egg running down
our shell-shocked faces,

pretty pink and green shards
nestled in our hair,

mouths agape like baby birds,
super-glued to our chairs,

until laughter scrambled
with our tears.

DEAR COFFEE

All the other times I've tried to leave, I've come
crawling back, but this time I mean it, things have
gone too far. Granted, I may not be thinking as
clearly without you by my side, but you can really get
on a person's nerves, and when I think of the nights
of high anxiety, the stomachaches you've given me,
my insane cravings for your strong embrace, it's no
wonder we've been on-again/off-again for years.

Herbal? Tea? you snort contemptuously. *You'll find
no passion there!* Okay, maybe I do want to play it
safe but I need a lover who treats me right, does no
harm, can ease me into sleep, gives me room to
meditate.

Java, my darling, you old charmer, there is no one
who smells as good as you first thing in the morning,
and it's true you always make my heart beat faster,
but please don't look at me that way you do, begging
me (at my age!) to stay up and dance with you until
four. No, no more. Here's your hat.

There's the door.

DISPATCH

Dear Cousin
writing to say
please don't come

we're ashamed
how far the old place
slants off to the right

it's a sham
a tumbledown false front
with busted-out windows

it's because of the sinkhole
we keep falling in
dig ourselves out again

go to the mall
where it's easier to pretend
everything's just fine here

the way it always was
down here in the States
we're united in denial

covered in mud.

DEADBOLT

I thought
I knew you, Deadbolt,
you and your kind: ubiquitous,
perhaps a bit
ridiculous in your
old-fashioned solid brass civility.
I mistook
your silence for simplicity,
assumed the quick rhythm of
your click-click-snap
meant
on or off,
unambiguous,
nothing
in-between.

But lately
I have begun to notice
your complexity,
the artful elegance of
our exchange: how I climb
each step
to where you
wait,
patient as a sphinx,
the way
I come
before you,
bowing my head.
In my hands
my endless questions
take the
shapes of
keys.

ANDROMEDA'S DAUGHTER

I was angry with my mother
back when she was a woman
chained to her shopping cart
like Andromeda to her rock.

I walked behind, a sullen spy
in someone else's court,
her exhausted walk
my first close-up look at lack.

Her stingy shoes clicked in time
with the one wobbly wheel,
making a jarring tune
I wanted to never learn.

She seemed a drudge
bludgeoned into service,
a cowering dog
drifting toward traffic.

How I hated her then
and the endless list
she clenched in her fist,
but it was that metal cart

I loathed most of all, the way it,
after the groceries were put away,
folded in on itself with a snap,
and into the corner was hung.

OUR JUST DESSERTS

Any thought or dream or game
She might interrupt with a scream
an abrupt command
the back of Her hand
or a cutting remark
with its whipsmart crack
but the way She communicated best
was in a secret regal code
that somehow matched Her cocktail dress.

The lightning-quick snap
of Her long manicured fingers was like
a lock clapping shut
and the *tsk* of Her tongue
could send a lick of ice-white flame
across the room
to the back of our necks.
We knew what it meant:
stopwhatyouredoingthisveryinstant.

When She made those sharp sounds
we were all of a sudden in
Big Trouble land again
no ifs ands or buts about it
some thoughtless thing we'd done
or maybe nothing at all
had sparked that match
but who ever knew what might offend
the tight-lipped Queen?

Yet worst of all were those days
Her face like a slammed door
stayed closed and She would not deign
to use our now-damned names.
That was the blow that could
strike right through
the toughest skin
into the smallest
hidden heart.

THE INVISIBLE GRIMOIRE

Now that I'm a Crone-Cook
vegetables tell me what to do
but chicken, fish, beef,
being dead, stay silent.
That's when my mother comes in.
She's dead too, but there's no stopping her,
the kitchen witch.

This is the woman
who ate raw hamburger
laced with pungent onion —
poor woman's steak tartare
she called it — winking and waggling
her long scarlet fingers at me like feathers,
all *la di da.*

Now her hand shakes
as she wings pink rock salt,
coarse black pepper, smashed white garlic
into my cast-iron pan, turning
the blue flame up on high
to flash-sear the meat, fast —
the way the ancestors must have done it.

A peripatetic people, often on the run,
hunted, haunted, vilified,
adaptive, inventive, able to craft
something out of almost nothing;
their hand-me-down recipes
best learned by heart,
encoded in the blood.

The Dead in my kitchen
chant one of their old incantations.
I hear it in my mother's voice
but I don't join them.
Instead I write it down,
my culinary tip of the day:

If you want to keep
the inside tender,
you have to risk the burning.

LAMENT

Breasts after 60 seem tired,
piqued, bored with it all,

drifting into a state of ennui.
After all the gravity they've defied,

they've good reason to crawl
like a couple of eggs

sunny side up
sliding off a plate.

A, B, C, or D cup,
breasts after 60 fall out

like estranged sisters
locked in stalemate,

each one sprawled
on her side of their bed of ribs,

won't look each other
in the eye as they debate

the merits of solitary retreat.

Port and starboard flagging,
Breasts after 60 semaphore

their intent to sail south
for the winter season

(a transparent lie,
everyone knows

they'll take up permanent
residence down there).

Breasts after 60 flatter
themselves, remembering

how they used to
spring up with a shout,

now they try and slip
unnoticed beneath armpits,

take a peek at what's
coming up from the rear.

Breasts after 60
are so outta here,

waving (buh-bye...
buh-bye...)

from a distant shore.

MY SUGGESTION FOR

THE HALL OF EXTINCTION

In addition to your very fine display
of taxidermied passenger pigeons,
kindly provide a variety
from your exquisite collection
of hand-blown glass vials,
so valued by the Egyptians,
later favored by the Victorians —

tear-catchers for us mourners,
one for each glass coffin.

NEEDLE

DON'T SAY I DIDN'T WARN YOU

If the next person to say they don't believe
in global warming is you,
if you tell me climate change isn't real,
isn't right here and now,
I will ask you to be quiet,
to keep your already-closed eyes shut
so you can listen to the sound of my voice
as I guide you in this meditation:

Imagine you're a young child who's been given
the best seat at a grand parade —
riding high atop the broad shoulders
of a genuine five-star war hero.

Happily you wave your little plastic flag
and all the pretty people on fantastic floats
wave back at you. There are big balloons,
crisp marching bands, drum corps, and silly clowns
making everyone laugh, all tumbling by,
        end over end,
under a rainbow confetti sky,

When all the while
    Behind you
        In the alley
            The general's troops
                Take turns
                    Raping and kicking
                    Your mother
                        To death.

VISIT TO THE UNOPTIMISTIC OPTOMETRIST

In the chilly examining room
all of the good doctor's implements
are cold and moist,

even the instrument of his voice

as he unapologetically states
*the fact is, ma'am, at your age, that duct
no longer works right in your left eye.*

But you could tell him why.

The day and night you cried out
all the tears of your life into
the empty side of the bed,

that's what unbalanced your head.

You suspect he will not agree
with the logic of your self-diagnosis,
the efficacy of home remedies:

laughter, carrots, herbal teas.

Another course of antibiotics is all
he can suggest plus frequent
periods of eye rest.

He refers you back to the front desk.

You nod as if you agree but silently
pledge to consult a wiser source
for a follow-up look-see:

the nearest Weeping Willow tree.

YOUR CONTRACT

We have taken the liberty.
You need do nothing.
Your signature is on file.
Consent is implied.

You need do nothing.
Our pledge ironclad.
Consent is implied.
On the bottom line.

Our pledge ironclad.
We mean business.
On the bottom line.
Guaranteed airtight.

We mean business.
Your happiness our priority.
Guaranteed airtight.
We render results.

Your happiness our priority.
On your behalf.
We render results.
Actions are being taken.

On your behalf.
Refer to your copy.
Actions are being taken.
For your protection.

Refer to your copy.
Conveniently shrink-wrapped.
For your protection.
The future is here.

Conveniently shrink-wrapped.
Your signature is on file.
The future is here.
We have taken the liberty.

A Wild Bird of Prey Among

The Docile Fowl

How proud she was to pass,
a sham Mother Hen

as she preened her feathered nest,
but never could she resist

the sudden hawkish peck
to the back of the neck

of her greedy, noisy brood,
so she picked the weakest one,

the runt with the clouded eye,
born from a paper-thin shell,

heckled it to death,
then fed its pale flesh to us,

her stronger chicks,
and we grew.

Still, none of us
ran past the yard,

or learned how
to use wings.

Not one of us ever flew.

WHAT THE BROOM HAD TO SAY

My sister the Carpet-Sweeper
Shamelessly, famously,
Lay down with
Old Scratch himself,

Then gave birth to
Their whiny brat,
His name so apt,
Little Dirt Devil.

His unholy racket
Frightens the dogs and cats
Gobbling everything down
His black-hole mouth.

But I, gentle besom,
Like Martha to Mary,
Am mum as I sweep up
The mess he leaves behind.

ODE TO ORDINARY THINGS

Let's give a big hand to
safety pins and paper clips,
sturdy button thread,
the twisty valve caps on tires,
zipper teeth that meet and match,
the tiny screws in eyeglass stems,
brilliantly tenacious Velcro.

Wondrous inventions,
steadfast servants,
always offstage, never destined
for the spotlight,
no fifteen minutes of fame.
More obvious when absent,
we feel betrayed if they fail us,
replace them and immediately forget,
or curse them, call them useless or worse.

Broken shoelaces flinch beneath our wrath.
Junk drawers, familiar with our harsh
interrogation techniques,
slam themselves shut,
refuse to reveal where we last put
the blasted *whatchamacallit*.

But in Japan, seamstresses
bring their old needles and pins,
nippers and scissors
to temples and shrines
for Hari-Kuyo,
the Festival of Broken Needles.

The women gently place their tools
into soft beds of tofu and jelly cakes,
offering prayers of gratitude
for their years of devotion and hard work.
They wrap them in soft silk cloths,
and bury them for a well-deserved rest.

I don't know the right ceremony,
don't have the correct words
for the blessings, so I say
thank you Pen. Thank you Spoon.
Thank you Nail, Thumbtack,
Knife, Hammer, Pencil
sharpened down to a nub.
Thank you all.

Broken Cup, in your memory,
I will sing a lullaby
to the next woebegone sock
in the street I see,
looking for its mate, lost,
so far from home.

A GARMENT WORKER'S SONG

— origin unknown

Pins and needles
Put to bed,
Shuttle's sleeping,
Feed dogs fed.

Pattern spread,
Fabric pinned,
Bobbins wound,
Scraps are binned.

Pins and needles
Put to bed,
Shuttle's sleeping,
Feed dogs fed.

Zippers quiet,
Hooks with eyes,
Scissors shut,
Knots all tied.

Shuttle's sleeping,
Feed dogs fed,
Pins and needles
Put to bed.

PERNOCTATION

— for Sam

If I hear
the great thwap of wings
as Death swoops down, claws extended,
will I run like a little mouse,
frantic from spot to spot,
vainly seeking escape?

Or will I pause,
pull in one more sweet breath,
stretch myself up to watch the fireflies
in their binary dance
become the stars
at last?

HOW I WANT YOU TO THINK OF ME

WHEN I'M GONE

Consider me Umbrella —
your classic British bumbershoot,
bella sombre in midnight blue dress,
playful parasol's sturdy cousin,
descendent of the humble
broad Palm leaf.

My mother was a wood-ear mushroom,
my father a bat on the wing,
and I, their exquisitely odd progeny.

Past the threshold,
that's where *I* flower.
Pinwheeling up from
fluted walking stick
to cartoon thought-cloud
hovering over your head.

Until then, I wait by the front door
in my cylindrical metal stand,
keeping all your secrets safe.

With a silver flash of wit
at my tip, I wink to remind you:
before you go, don't forget to
remember me.
Remember me, remember me.
Remember.

Acknowledgments

Grateful acknowledgment to the editors of the following publications in which these poems, or earlier versions of them, originally appeared:

Andromeda's Daughter /*The Cause of Crows* 2019 Budlong Writers Annual Anthology "Knickknacks & Tchotchkes"

Deadbolt 2016 – Video poem by Paul Broderick https://vimeo.com/126632400

Deadbolt / *Eat Up the Stars* / *In Memoriam* 2015 – PoetryStoreHouse.com

Dear Coffee 2018 – Highland Park Poets Muses Gallery "Coffee, Tea and Other Beverages"

Eat Up the Stars 2018 –"The Stars"; *The Park Closes at Night* 2019 –"Loon Magic and Other Night Sounds" TallGrass Writers' Black & White Anthology

My Mother's Keepsakes 2019 – Poetry Foundation/Chicago Seniors Poetry Publication

Pernoctation 2016 / *Easter Eggs for Lunch* 2019 / *The Park Closes at Night* 2019 – YourDailyPoem.com

Awards

giddy up girl 2013 / *Pernoctation* 2016 – Jo-Anne
Hirshfield Memorial Poetry Awards

How I Want You to Think of Me When I'm Gone 2014 /
My Suggestion for the Hall of Extinction 2016 – Poets &
Patrons Annual Contest

Adapted for Stage

Ode to Ordinary Things / *Book Club* 2014 – Rhinoceros
Fringe Theater Festival, FourTell Performance Group
"Somewhere Under the Table"

Stella Maris 1993 Links Hall / 1994 Chicago Center for
Book & Paper Arts / 1995 Synergy Gallery for the Arts

Appreciation

My sincere gratitude and thanks to Doug Chamberlin, Anara Guard, Sam Guard, David Hutchinson, the Interplay Community, Michelle Klee, Illinois State Poetry Society, Chloe F. Orwell, Donna Pecore & the Budlong Writers, Caroline Johnson & Poets & Patrons, Maggie Queeney of the Poetry Foundation & the North Center Seniors Poetry Group, Whitney Scott & the TallGrass Writers, and Women on the Verge.

For dear friends now on the other side of my book club: Zuberi Badili, Danna Ephland, Larry Norwood, and Susie Redmond. Warrior-artists and mentors, may your memory be a blessing always.

About the Author

Gay Guard Chamberlin is a writer, performance artist and multi-media visual artist. A graduate of Columbia College, Chicago, with a Masters in Interdisciplinary Arts, Gay is a member of Poets & Patrons, Illinois State Poets Society, TallGrass Writers Guild, Budlong Writers Group, North Center Seniors Poetry Group sponsored by the Poetry Foundation, and Women on the Verge in Kalamazoo, MI.

She has taught skills as diverse as self-defense/martial arts and paper-making to children and adults, and is a certified Interplay instructor. Gay has also worked as an office manager for an arts-in-schools organization, a waitress, childcare provider, and caregiver for people with dementia.

She lives on the North side of Chicago with her husband, musician-artist Doug Chamberlin. *Red Thread Through a Rusty Needle* is her first book.

About New Wind Publishing

New Wind Publishing is a small independent press located in Sacramento, California.

We believe in the craft of writing, the importance of books, and the ability of the written word to express truth, convey beauty, and change lives. We work closely and collaboratively with each writer through the stages of bringing a book to life.

If you have enjoyed this book, you may also enjoy *Hand on My Heart*, poems by Anara Guard (ISBN 978-1-929777-13-6). Gay and Anara perform their poetry together as "Sibling Revelry."

Visit www.NewWindPublishing.com to learn more, or request any of our books from your favorite local bookstore.